IF YOU CAN DRAW THESE THINGS →
YOU WILL BE ABLE TO DRAW
ALL THE THINGS IN THIS BOOK.

△ △ ∧ S ⌣
▢ ⊓ . ∖ ww
◯ C D

FOR INSTANCE ——

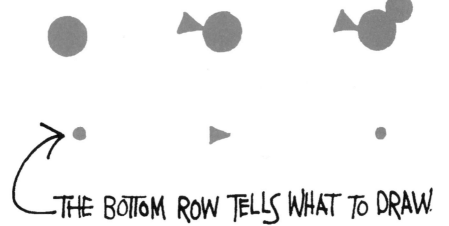

THE BOTTOM ROW TELLS WHAT TO DRAW.

THE TOP ROW TELLS WHERE TO PUT IT.

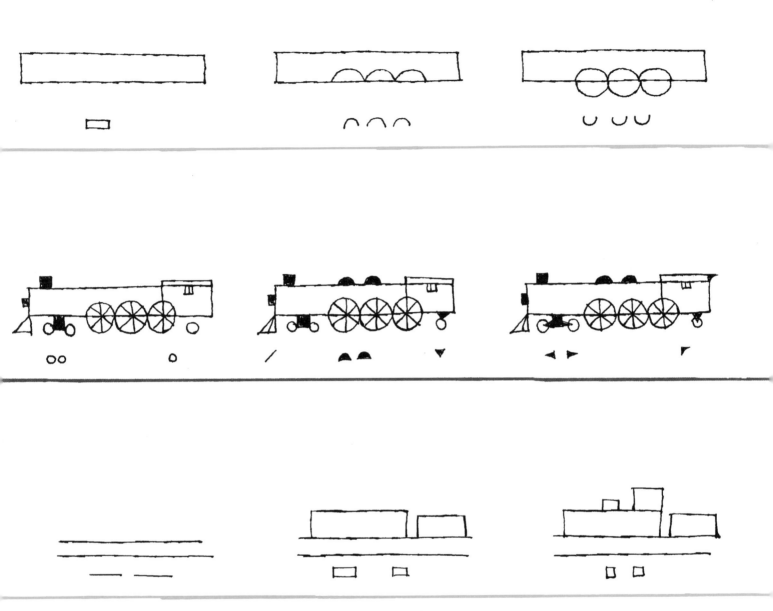

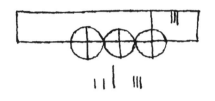

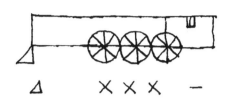

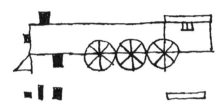

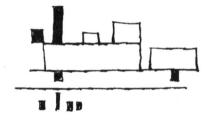

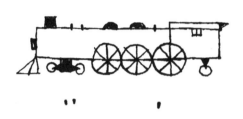

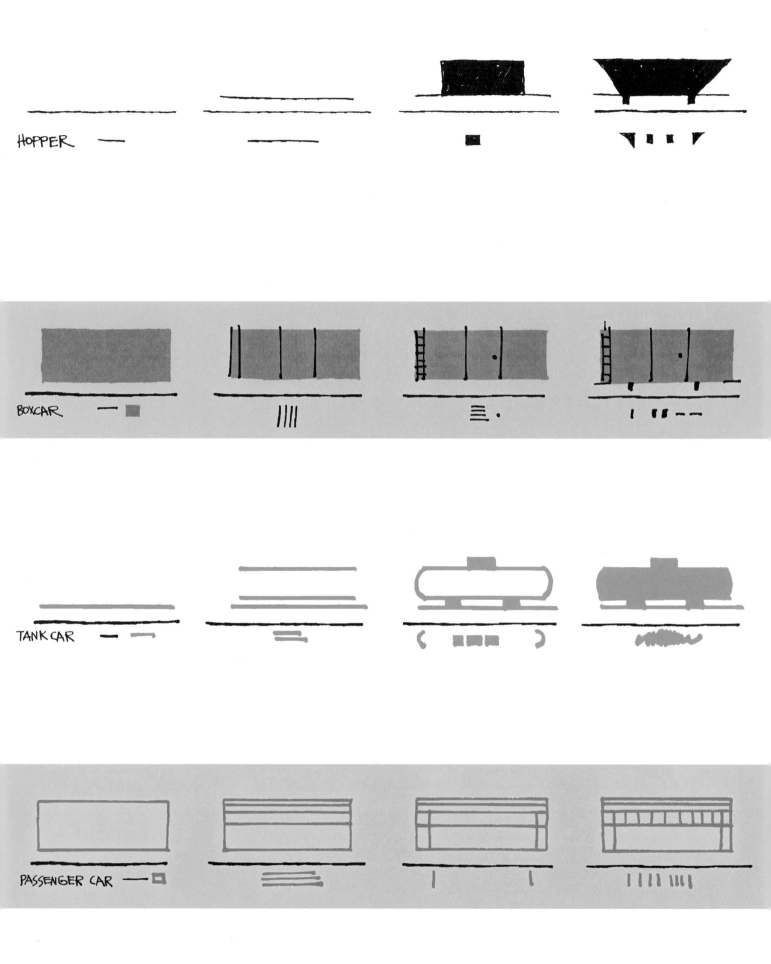

HOPPER

BOXCAR

TANK CAR

PASSENGER CAR

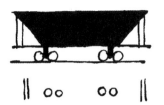   

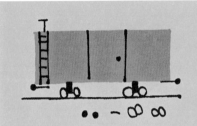   

DOOR OPEN

N.H.
R.R.

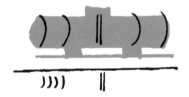 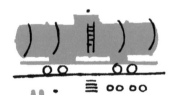 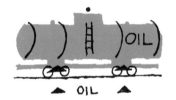 

OIL

MILK

  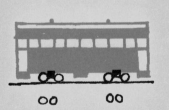 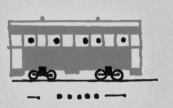

STOCK CAR

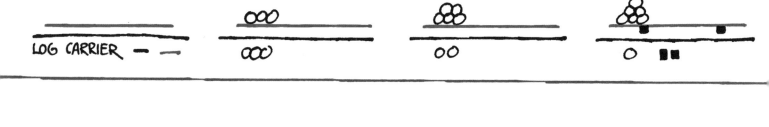

LOG CARRIER

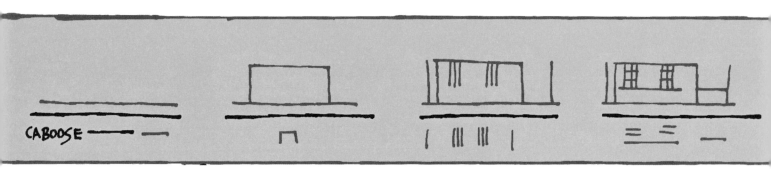

CABOOSE

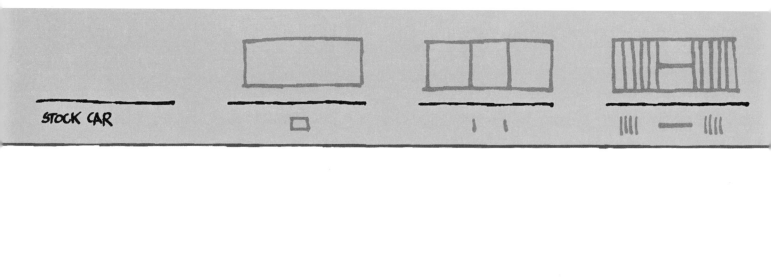

OIL

STUFF

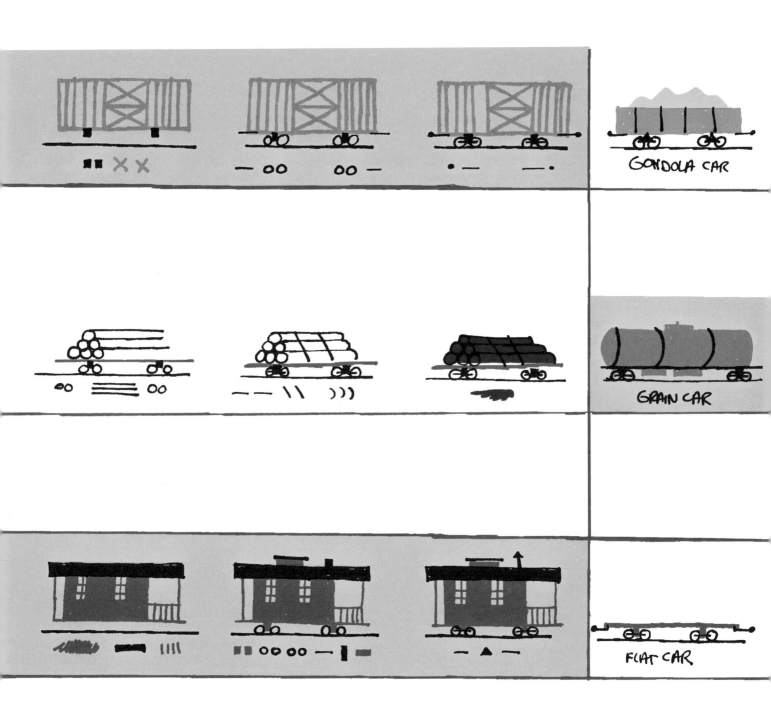

GONDOLA CAR

GRAIN CAR

FLAT CAR

EGGS

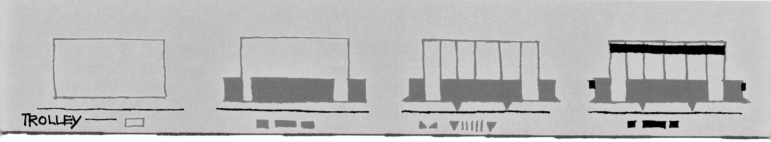

TROLLEY

COAL TENDER

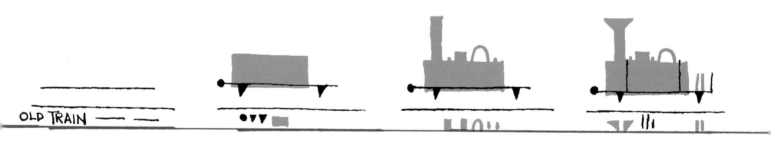

OLD TRAIN

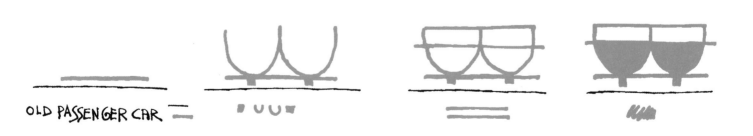

OLD PASSENGER CAR

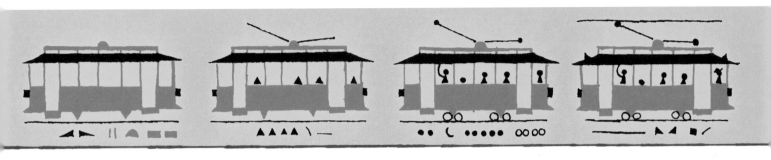

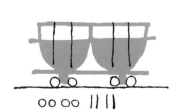

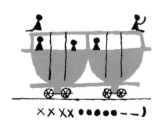

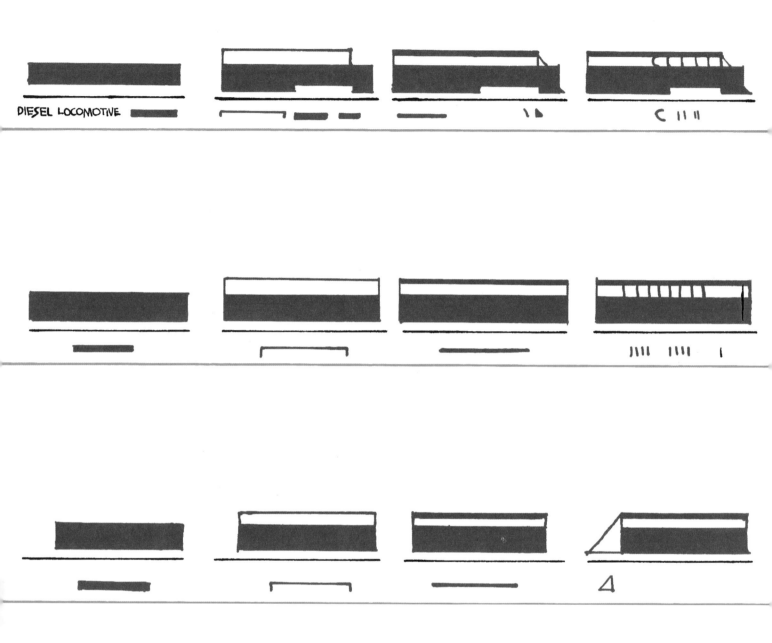

DIESEL LOCOMOTIVE

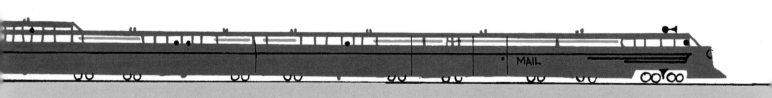

MAIL

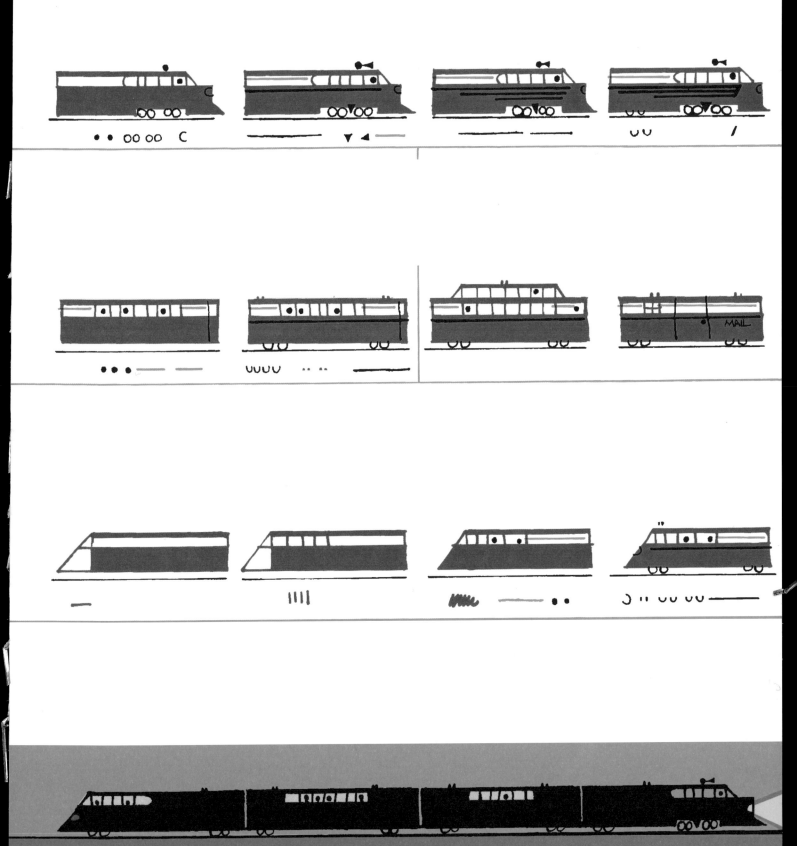

MAIL

BAGGAGE CART

PASSENGERS

STATION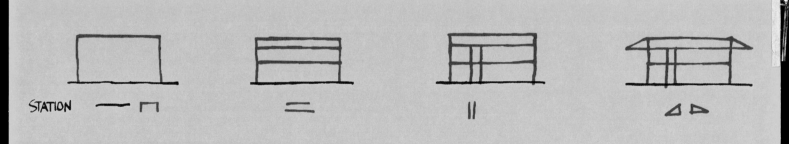

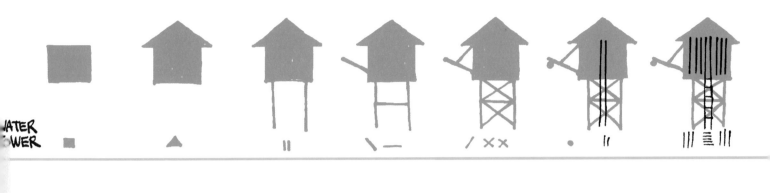

WATER
TOWER

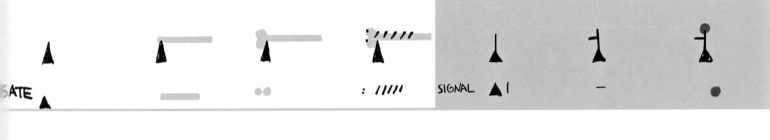

GATE

SIGNAL

GATE
MAN

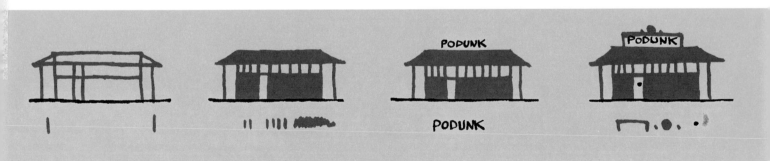

PODUNK

PODUNK

PODUNK

PODUNK

PICKUP TRUCKS

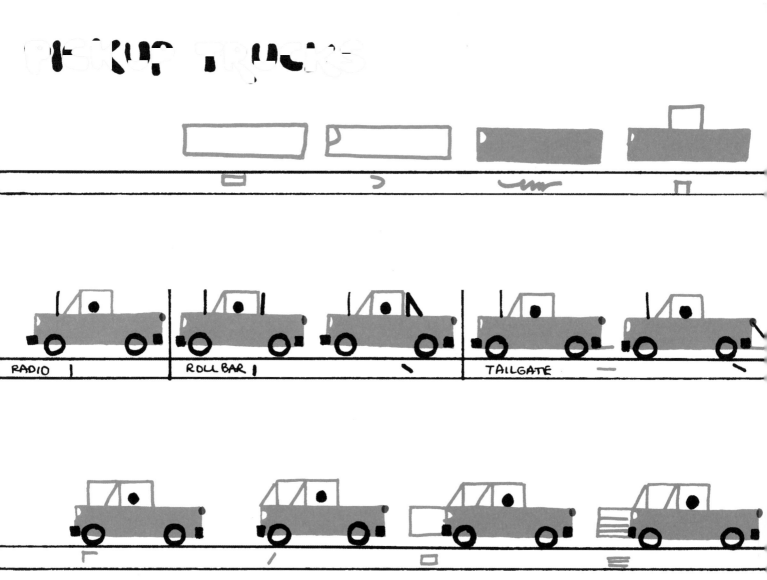

RADIO | ROLL BAR | TAILGATE

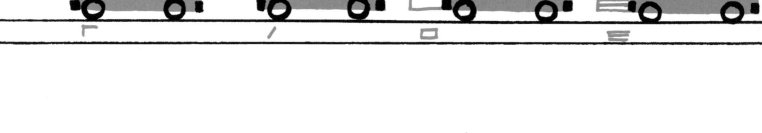

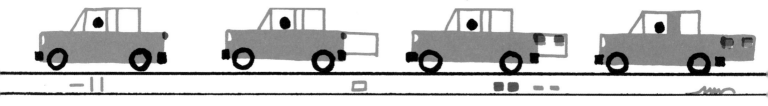

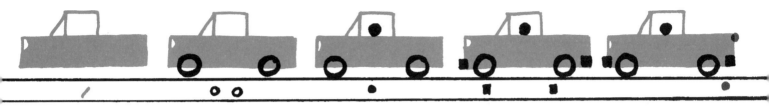

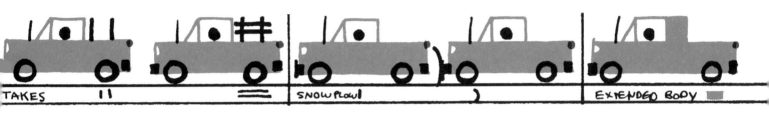

TAKES   11   ≡   SNOWPLOW!   )   EXTENDED BODY

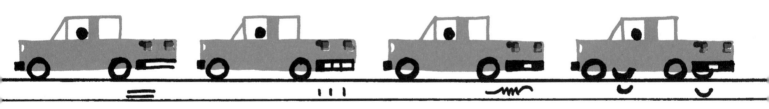

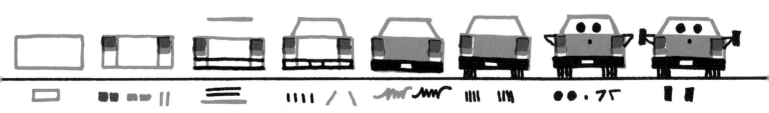

PANELTRUCK CAP = II

HAY DIRT WOOD DOG

CAMPER

COMPETITION

18

TOOL BOX ▬ BIG TOOL BOX ☐ ∿ LADDER | |

// •• ••• PIGS ●● ▲▲▲ •• •• ▲▲

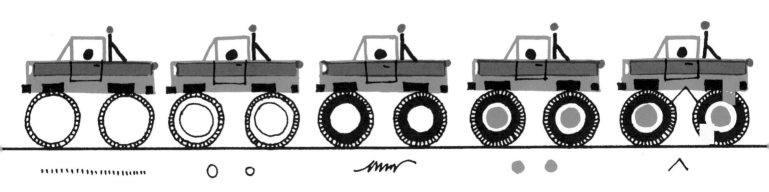

O o ∿ ●● ∧

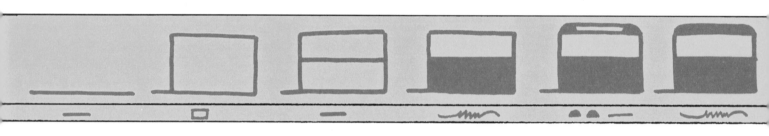

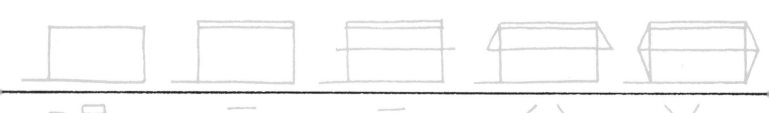

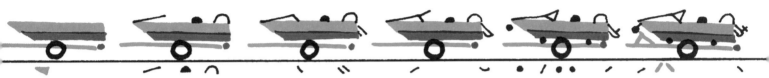

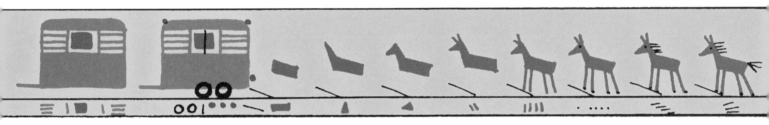

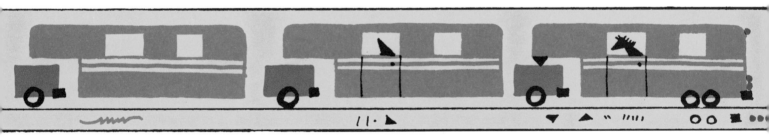

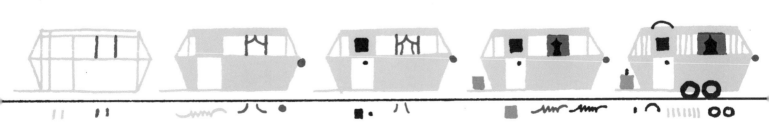

VANS

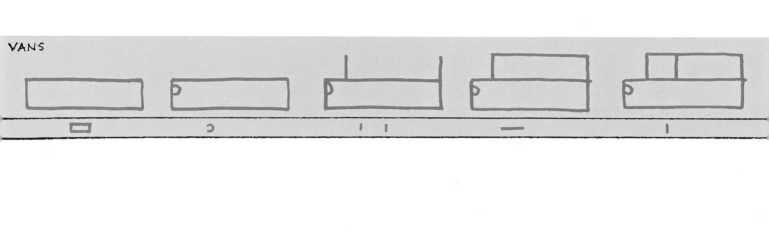

PASSENGER VAN

FIX IT

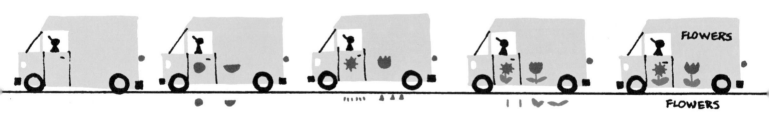

FLOWERS

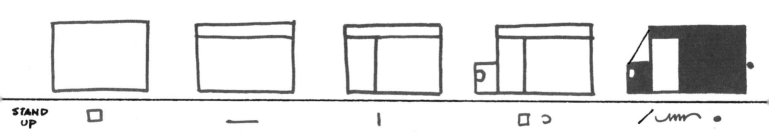

STAND UP

22

LONG BODY ⊐   ■ ∿ ●   HIGH ROOF ———   / | ∿

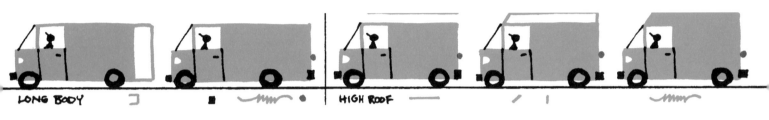

FISH

     • ⌣ FISH

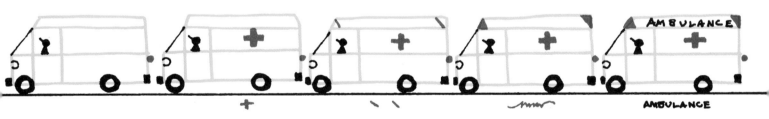

AMBULANCE

     +   ∿   AMBULANCE

US MAIL

■ ○ ▬ ○ ■   ◢ ◣   • ▲ \   // //   ▬ — — US MAIL

HEAVY TRUCKS

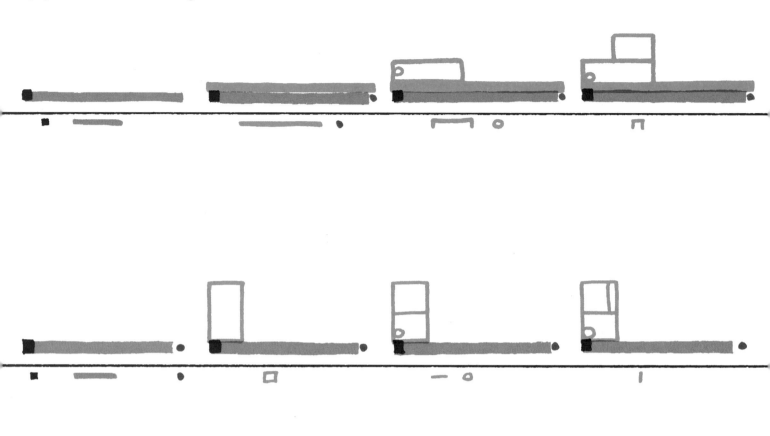

BED CAN BE SHORT   OR LONG   AND THIS FLATBED TRUCK CAN CARRY ALL SORTS OF THINGS

TOYS   ICE CREAM   ACME MOVERS

LOGS

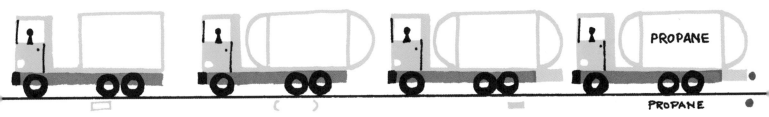

PROPANE

PROPANE

CEMENT

CEMENT ·

TRASH

TRASH

TOW

TOW

ADD TRUCK

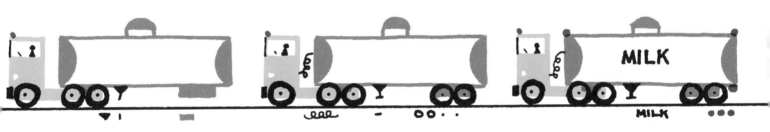

SLEEPING CAB ◗

AIR HORN   D —

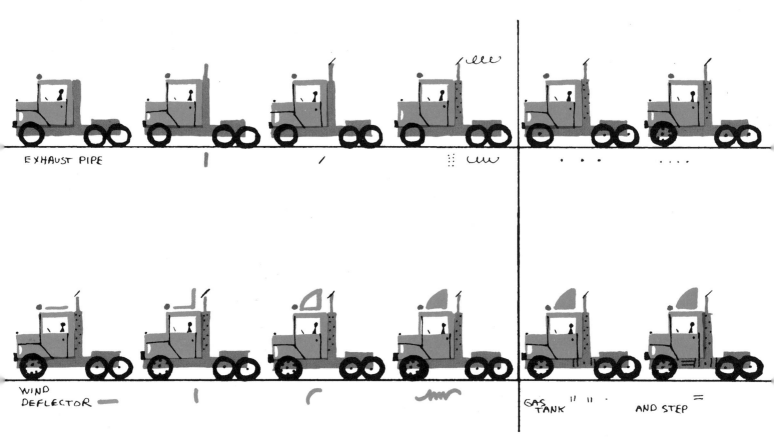

EXHAUST PIPE

WIND
DEFLECTOR —

GAS
TANK " "
AND STEP   =